Theory Paper Grade 3   2013   A
Model Answers

1 (10)

2 *There are many ways of completing this question. The specimen completion below would receive full marks.* (10)

3 (10)

4 (10)

5 (10)

6 (10)

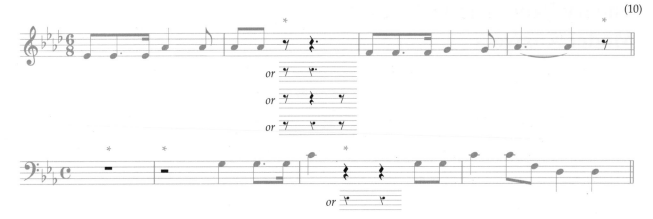

7 F melodic minor (10)
   B♭ major
   A major
   E harmonic minor

8 (a) at a walking pace / medium speed (10)
84 crotchets in a minute / 84 quarter notes in a minute / 84 crotchet beats in a minute /
    84 quarter-note beats in a minute
much / very
expressive / expressively / with expression
getting quieter / gradually getting quieter

(b) (10)

(i)

(ii) C♯
(iii) melodic
(iv) *legato* (smoothly)
(v) simple
triple

(c) (10)

4

Music Theory Past Papers 2013

Model Answers

ABRSM Grade 3

Welcome to ABRSM's *Music Theory Past Papers 2013 Model Answers*, Grade 3. These answers are a useful resource for students and teachers preparing for ABRSM theory exams and should be used alongside the relevant published theory past papers.

All the answers in this booklet would receive full marks but not all possible answers have been included for practicable reasons. In these cases other reasonable alternatives may also be awarded full marks. For composition-style questions (where candidates must complete a rhythm, compose a melody based on a given opening or set text to music) only one example of the many possible answers is given.

For more information on how theory papers are marked and some general advice on taking theory exams, please refer to the Music Theory Grade 3 web page: www.abrsm.org/theory3.

Using these answers

- Answers are given in the same order and, where possible, in the same layout as in the exam papers, making it easy to match answer to question.

- Where it is necessary to show the answer on a stave, the original stave is printed in grey with the answer shown in black, for example:

- Alternative answers are separated by an oblique stroke (/) or by *or*, for example:

    getting slower / gradually getting slower

- Answers that require the candidate to write out a scale or chord have been shown at one octave only. Reasonable alternatives at different octaves can also receive full marks.

© 2014 by The Associated Board of the Royal Schools of Music
Published by ABRSM (Publishing) Ltd, a wholly owned subsidiary of ABRSM
Cover by Kate Benjamin & Andy Potts
Printed in England by Page Bros (Norwich) Ltd

Theory Paper Grade 3   2013   B
Model Answers

1      (10)

2   *There are many ways of completing this question. The specimen completion below would receive full marks.*   (10)

3   (10)

(a)

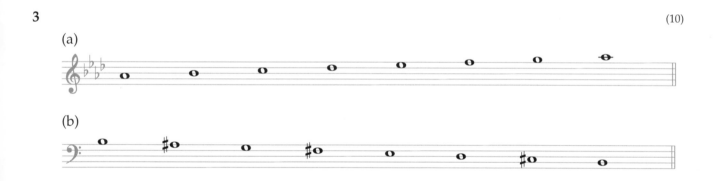

(b)

4   (10)

5   (10)

6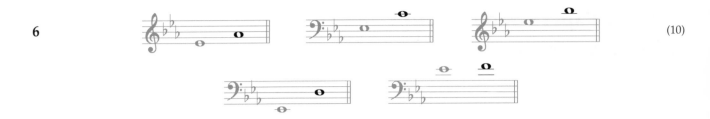

(10)

7

(10)

Elgar

8 (a)   at a walking pace / medium speed (10)
simple / plain
quiet / soft
always / ever
held back / getting slower / gradually getting slower

(b) (10)

(i)   five
(ii)   4 / last bar
(iii) A minor
(iv)   compound
       duple
(v)   6th

(c) (10)

Theory Paper Grade 3 2013 C
Model Answers

1 (10)

2 *There are many ways of completing this question. The specimen completion below would receive full marks.* (10)

3 (10)

4 minor   perfect   major (10)
   6th   4th   7th

       perfect   minor
        5th   3rd

5 (10)

6 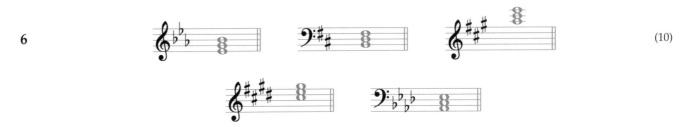 (10)

7 (10)

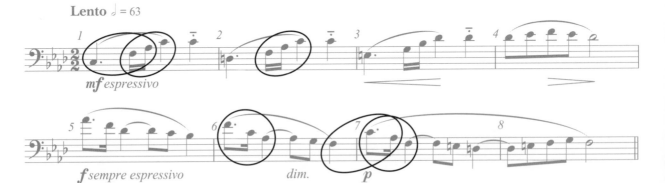

8 (a) slow (10)

63 minims in a minute / 63 half notes in a minute / 63 minim beats in a minute / 63 half-note beats in a minute

expressive / expressively / with expression

getting quieter / gradually getting quieter

always / ever

(b) (10)

(i) *There are six possible answers to this question. Any of the answers shown would receive full marks.*

Lento ♩ = 63

mf espressivo

f sempre espressivo   *dim.*   *p*

(ii) false

    true

(iii) *legato* (smoothly)

(iv) A♭

(c)   (10)

Theory Paper Grade 3   2013   S
Model Answers

1   (10)

etc.

Britten

etc.

2   *There are many ways of completing this question. The specimen completion below would receive full marks.*   (10)

3   B♭ major   A major   C minor   (10)

       E minor   C♯ minor

4   (10)

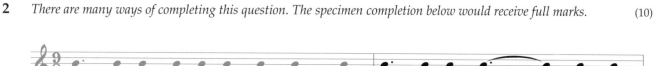

5 (10)

etc.

6 (10)

major	perfect	perfect
7th	5th	4th

major	minor
2nd	6th

7 (10)

8 (a) (10)

  (i)   fast / quick / cheerful / lively
        majestic / stately
        116 crotchets in a minute / 116 quarter notes in a minute / 116 crotchet beats in a minute /
            116 quarter-note beats in a minute
        always / ever

  (ii)   simple
        quadruple

 (b) (10)

  (i)   5th

  (ii)

  (iii) Similarity   melodic shape / rhythm
         Difference   pitch / dynamics

  (iv)

  (v)   16

(c)  (10)

Music Theory Past Papers 2013 Model Answers

Model answers for four past papers from ABRSM's 2013 Theory exams for Grade 3

Key features:
- a list of correct answers where appropriate
- a selection of likely options where the answer can be expressed in a variety of ways
- a single exemplar where a composition-style answer is required

Support material for ABRSM Theory exams

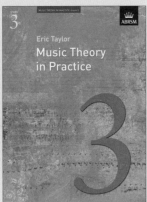

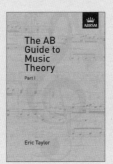

ABRSM
24 Portland Place
London W1B 1LU
United Kingdom

www.abrsm.org

ABRSM is the exam board of the Royal Schools of Music. We are committed to actively supporting high-quality music-making, learning and development throughout the world, and to producing the best possible resources for music teachers and students.

ISBN 978-1-84849-616-3

9 781848 496163